Also By Michael Salcman

Crossing The Tape

poems

Michael Salcman

SPUYTEN DUYVIL
New York City

© 2024 Michael Salcman
ISBN 978-1-959556-99-2

cover image © Leon Polk Smith Foundation;
Courtesy Lisson Gallery. Photography by Elisabeth Bernstein.

Leon Polk Smith
Correspondence: Deep Yellow-Green, 1967
Acrylic on canvas
121 cm diameter x 2.5 cm
47 5/8 in diameter x 1 in
(SMIL670005)

Library of Congress Cataloging-in-Publication Data

Names: Salcman, Michael, author.
Title: Crossing the tape / Michael Salcman.
Other titles: Crossing the tape (Compilation)
Description: New York City : Spuyten Duyvil, 2024.
Identifiers: LCCN 2024003847 | ISBN 9781959556992 (paperback)
Subjects: LCGFT: Poetry.
Classification: LCC PS3569.A45924 C76 2024 | DDC 811/.54--dc23/eng/20240129
LC record available at https://lccn.loc.gov/2024003847

CORRESPONDENCE: DEEP YELLOW-GREEN
—after a tondo by Leon Polk Smith, 1967

There are only two possibilities:
Either the shadow of an orange sun has fallen
On the green earth or
An orange moon is partially occluded
By a green sun;
Either the orange scimitar is turning
Around a green ball
Or the ball is spinning out of an orange disc.
Either everything is moving or everything is still.
There are only two possibilities.

CONTENTS

III—BODY & BRAIN

IV—EKPHRASIS

V—IN TWILIGHT

I

BEGINNINGS

"…love is a form of intelligence—a way of listening to the world, of taking it in, of rising above one's angry heart."—
Alfred Kazin (diary entry re: Shirley Hazzard)

THE LONG MOMENT

I have kept my ear against the sky
forever and ever
where the radiant past of a distant star
with the faintest signal from another galaxy
seems to say here we are
shake hands with your relatives,
lovers and friends,
and the light of that star will catch you up
with the past when the present evaporates.

Of the future nothing is known
but the past is certain, banked in ledgers
and journals, and shining in our lenses
on mountaintops from light years away.
After the Sun grows cold
the planets of a more distant star
will see us on our return
and hear our voices in their telepathy.
Our past is their future, its music and film
and the thin line of our poetry—Take care.

THE RAINBOW IS THE ENEMY OF ENVY

—after Olafur Eliasson

Its generosity lies in its unexpected appearance
on a city corner or at the edge of the ocean,
the position of the sun, the humidity of the air
and the attention of our eyes perfectly aligned,
each one uniquely coddling a spectrum in red,
orange, green, blue, an indigo and violet,
a momentary experiment like a kiss on an eyelid.

A rainbow is actually a circle and you would see it
whole if there were no horizon blocking the view
and you stood at its center in place of the earth.
Delaunay discovered his circles in just that way
by removing anything arrogant enough to compete
just to the side of where you have come to stand,
your own eyes freed of permanency and possession.

DINOSAURS & POLIO, 1952

Seeing into the past I feel the small gray stegosaurus
        wind between my fingers like a cat,
its row of dorsal plates like dragon teeth,
        whipping a three-pronged club at the end of its tail
as it slips from a box of Nabisco Wheat-Honeys
        chasing a slime green brontosaurus until
the two reptiles shake in four-legged stances on my sheets
        partially balanced by their heavy bellies.

Chewing on their memory brings back the taste
        of cheap injection molding, how I inhaled the neon dyes
that made them less than perfect and all that excess trim:
        the satanic tail of a flying pterodactyl melted
into outstretched wing, the cancerous bulges
        on the occipital shield of a triceratops
and most of all in my six-year-old brain
        a tyrannosaurus dressed in electric blue or lipstick red.

These Mesozoic monsters crawled across my useless legs
        for six months, like Technicolor ants tramping
on a new Gulliver tied up
        without a proper snare.
Frankenstein might have said, "they're alive, they're alive"
        but they never grew, turning strangely dead
while my body's asymmetry grew even as I swept
        extinct shapes and cartoon colors out of my head.

THE VOICE OF SUMMER—Vin Scully

The voice of baseball
Was the voice of my youth
It took up residence in my head—
I didn't know then it was the voice of poetry
Built in its pauses.

When Koufax pitched his perfect game
The voice of summer said in Brooklyn
There are 29,000 fans in the stands
(pause)
And a million butterflies.

In mind and ear his voice shared a space
With my mother born the very same year
She who fell silent more than fifty years before
The voice of summer did.

Soon after we had a black and white TV set
The colors of this mild Irish tenor
Made for a theater of the mind
And the voice of nine-act operas.

Now there's an equality of sadness in my brain
From Old World sepia pictures
But no recordings of her voice
And no film or tape of him performing
The song of youth and the end of the game.

THE ENVELOPE

It must have started on this journey
in Arizona
thirty or forty years ago
well before it returned unmarked
in Baltimore holding
four or five carbon copies
of early poems
possibly found by a grieving family,
a brother or widow
who had assumed the mantle of duty
after cleaning out the basement
or a deceased editor's study.

Did they think I might miss
the hand-made copies made back then
with primitive technology
by a person I no longer knew,
mailing this mystery anonymously
without a return address
as if this kindness would console me
in the present,
as if the poems still had value
to someone I no longer recognized
just because these poems
of uncertain quality were mine?

Perhaps the family feared an endless loop
of unwanted return
from yet another cross-country trip
the despondent writer carefully counting
how many decades rejection took.

THE PAPER

Not a metaphor but an argument we are losing,
the haptic touch of poems and the books they sit in,

the hidden smell of glue and its slowly turning leaves
from trees reading out our seasons:

Turgenev's sled in snow, a chorale sung in spring,
a pressed summer flower and Cole Porter's Parisian Fall.

I'm wed to the codex, where the living world touches
the page and there's print I can kiss if I have a mind to

not some glass coffin behind which a mannequin greets
the pulsating tip of my finger. I eschew the electron

and its false promise of ease, writing in a lined journal
(hair growing gray in my nose, nails yellow with dirt)

with a reader like you in mind, sitting in a favorite chair
with a drink, the fire lit, and this little speech close at hand.

THE STACK

I apologize for not reading the stack of books you've sent me,
those wet stories of a West Virginia childhood
with nighttime drives around cliffs
between drunk-fests and other pranks,
not to mention the tomes on cats and ocean creatures
with glowing eyes
that now occupy the surface tops of tables
this foreign army stationed
in more than one room of my house.
I feel trapped by duty.

I promise you I will never catch up with the task;
I've got my own writing to do
and must read the books I need in order to write.
I'm not even counting the little time I've got left
for the words of friends who've asked the favor
of a blurb or two.

Be glad I'm not your ideal reader.
I fill up the hours
with the guilt of not clearing my desk—
my hypertrophied superego and overcritical morality
prevent me from closing the covers
of any book I open without finishing or thinking.

THE HOUSE IS A LADY
(No.1 *from* EIGHT ROOMS FOR AN OLD HOUSE)

Best seen by walking corridors and looking at the walls—
the narrow arteries of the halls force you to enter
a great lung-full of rooms with the sounds of talk, music and sleep,
and grand views of the lawn and streets.
By day the exterior view of the U-shaped house
is her glory, as if checking on herself in a mirror,
and seeing nothing and no one else,
a self-conscious brain of white-washed Maryland stone
and wood-framed windows dressed in green mascara.
At sundown she dons two rows of lights, a necklace
and crown brightening the bluestone pavers in front
of her face, the rounded courtyard and rarely opened mouth
stretched between a painted clown and a queen.

THE BRICKS OF BALTIMORE

Forty miles to Washington on Route 95,
        the bricks go South a truck at a time
in a funeral procession to their final rest
        in the false façades of other peoples' homes,
their faces power-washed and dried by hand.

In the apartment blocks of the rich the bricks
        of Baltimore are more than a painful metaphor
of how a city of wasps has sucked out the wealth
        from its darker sister like a carnivorous insect.

The city's ruination began when Beth Steel closed
        its giant plant at Sparrow's Point
and thirty-five thousand good paying jobs left us
        a town of spavined rowhouses with marble stoops
and neighborhoods emptied of workers.

You can guess their origin by a brick's color and heft:
        orange examples from a dumpster on Chase,
the oldest looking born on Federal Street and a few
        with vertical stripes from Fenwick Avenue.

The folks in DC condos are deaf to any rumors of a past,
        our old bricks serving for surface decoration
don't carry the weight of the walls as they once did
        when the national wealth was more equally spread
when the sixth largest city always had more, not less.

THE EGREGIOUS MEMORY PALACE OF DR. S—

Of my life I remember almost nothing. My memory palace has no drawing rooms only hooks on which to hang things and people like slabs of meat; it looks a lot like an apartment block in Beirut. I can always ask a childhood friend from Brooklyn, a poet as it happens, to tell me how I lived. This is how I remember the day my mother died six months before Picasso passed in 1973. She was a kind and intelligent woman no more important to the world than any other person but my culturally arrogant memory automatically tags her with someone big, someone I've actually spent a lot more time thinking about. Picasso. The day I heard how the wife of my best friend died by falling down the basement stairs and bleeding into her head I naturally thought of the violet snows of Pissarro or Monet and said so in a poem. It's a good thing my friend only reads non-fiction; boy would he be angry! The awful truth is I can't seem to order the world according to the ordinary. Does that make me a monster? Tell me if you remember where you were when Aunt Sadie or Uncle Ralph breathed their last or what you were doing when your father-in-law died in an Auckland car crash. If you can't it's because they're not fit subjects for cocktail chatter. But everyone above a certain age has to have an answer for where they were when J.F.K. died or the Towers fell. I was in college, sitting in physical chemistry, when they announced the death of the president and the class was cancelled and everyone stood up and marched out weeping. It took me a few moments to figure out why. As for the other, I was shaving late on a morning when my patient's surgery had been cancelled and turned on the television after a radio flash and saw the first plane hit the North Tower and knew immediately what and who had done it. It was a clear, clear day. Horror impresses memory like nothing else; emotion drives the hippocampus in your temporal lobe, the scratchpad of memory, seven chunks at a time. I can't imagine the poor person who has to make up answers to such questions, where were they when the motorcade passed the Book Depository in Dallas or what they were doing when the Towers collapsed in New York, sleeping? Their memory palace must look like North Avenue in Baltimore. Bet you don't know what you were about when Velcro was invented. I do. Some things just stick in the mind or not.

THE PROBLEM IS

I've been writing the same long poem for 132 years; an early draft was almost published but WWI put an end to that. This was well before open mics and local poets who performed from wrinkled sheets of paper for therapeutic reasons. The problem is I never had a chance to read my poem out loud in front of a real audience other than poets. But then I never could read a really long poem in front of twenty or thirty poets without watching them leave one at a time like the members of an orchestra in Haydn's Farewell Symphony. Most everyone knows the best strategy is to perform shorter poems, more musical verses or poems with a sense of humor. The problem is the poem I started before I was born is none of these things and the audience for it gradually disappeared during WWII. Soon after the war we had microphones and no one gave up their chance to read in front of an almost empty room. There's always too little time. And yet, I could never tell how good a poem was, whether short or long, if I didn't read it to someone other than a poet. On the other hand, I had no trust in the response I got from any audience because I'm too good a performer and reading out loud almost always makes people think a poem is better than it really is. After the Korean debacle, I spent more than fifty years polishing techniques for operating on the brain and lecturing on subjects like malignant tumors in the brain's erotic centers. I implanted microwave antennas for turning tumors into mush like Dairy Cream yogurt without seeds or nuts, you can bet those audiences stayed awake, responding to the slides with a hush, or a laugh or even applause. So, I couldn't turn poetry into books until after I retired. The problem is there are many more poets writing books than people reading them. I often felt like Ahab chasing the whale and then I died. The real problem is I finished writing the very long poem after I expired. A warning then to all my friends reading this complaint, you haven't read the big poem yet and I am not the whale.

A Day On The Big Island

Three generations gather together,
some drive off to the waterfalls,
others drown themselves in three feet
of ocean, knees laughing in the eddies
of schooling fish and tickled thighs,
the little children making sand castles,
the adults dissolving time.

My legs tremble and wobble
as little ones climb up my body
and cling to my neck,
their small arms dimpled with fat,
almost steal my breath,
their open mouthed rosy-pink laughs
and cheering lungs swaying my torso like fish.

It was the wrong season for watching whales
and I never saw a black crab against dark lava.
Where I swam, the fish seem borrowed
from the Caribbean: yellow tangs,
sergeant majors and parrotfish,
a few crustaceans with lobster-red legs
as shiny as lacquered tables.
                            And all around
the faded coral fingers lie burned gray
by chemicals and hot air.
No sponges or colored fans live to sweep
the water clean. I remove my mask.

HURRICANE ARTHUR

—for my father (1911-2010)

We sat like three statues at the edge of the lawn
as the knitting basket and green watering can
fell over in the stiff breeze blowing through
the pink dogwoods and the towering tulip poplars.

Far away, in Ocean City, gusty winds, high surf
and constant rain from the outer bands of the storm
made their way up the coast from Florida to Boston,
hitting my father's usual haunts, the old man
who shared a name with the season's first hurricane.

He'd also lent his voice, grown so loud and desperate
over time I almost failed to recognize it blowing
in our trees. So, he shook me like a whisk in a pan,
threw a branch, then another, before stopping to inhale,
crying *I am one with nature, look at what I have done.*

Mother At Eighty-Eight

In the obituaries I always look for those born in 1927
when my mother, a children's librarian, was born,
calculating how old she would be in any given year
if not for her early death at forty-six.

1927 was an interesting year—Ruth hit sixty
and a famous fascist flew across the Atlantic solo.
Mother did nothing similar but shaped me like a potter
making a bud vase or wine flask at the wheel.

Impelled by duty she threatened and cajoled me,
read a book or two every night, took me to museums
filled with the better things Europe had done
and not the worst.

I know almost nothing of her side of the family—
most names burnt by history had died before
the internet came to memorialize death
with an impervious stone made of electrons.

Since that day in 1973 I've never properly grieved
but every few years write her a note like this.

The Importance Of Measure

After the German war, my father worked
          as a top mechanical engineer at the Škoda Works
in Pilsen Czechoslovakia, where I was born
          and from which we escaped to America.
In New York he designed machines in which
          vertical stacks of lunch plates moved on springs
out of cylindrical tunnels one at a time.
          Strength and design were everything to him;
after retiring he moved his hand tools, table saw
          and milling machine into the garage
where he taught my son how to build things out
          of wood and metal, the importance of measure.

Though I had his good eye and preached precision,
          I managed to lose father's best vernier and caliper
between piles of books in my study. His favorite
          tool was made in his favorite material, hardened
stainless steel, produced in Japan before or after
          the war by Mitutoyo. Its two pairs of caliper jaws
used to measure the inner and outer diameters
          of hollow pipe on either the 15-centimeter metric scale
above or the six imperial inches below a central groove
          from which a thin finger of equal length can be extended
as needed to measure the inner depth of a tube.

A magical dial sits atop the vernier like an ugly clock
          or malevolent eye and lets you measure in hundredths
of an inch. Below its glass face a wedge of abraded paper
          makes the metal pan look covered in silver paint.
When I finally recovered this treasure, it still held oil
          in its rails my father had placed more than a decade ago,
and the force of his memory, the importance of measure.

POETIC LICENSE

I used to be on the other side the one with a scalpel
And someone else's brain seen through a microscope
I used to suffer from certainty but gave up my license
From age in my legs and my eyes.

I still have a permit as a poet the one with unread books
And very occasional acceptances
Taking allowance when writing letters to my love

Taking up various characters like an actor
Especially a crap salesman with a mouth full of samples.

I know where and how I'd gotten my medical license
But no memory of permission for me putting down
How life went on in my sort of century
Conditioned by horror and disbelief. You know—

It was our time and that's what is meant by poetic license.

II
OF WAR & VIOLENCE

The struggle of man against power is memory against forgetting
—Milan Kundera,
The Book of Laughter and Forgetting (1979)

Books On The Firing Range

It seemed like such a good idea at the time:
soldiers in the first World War thought they could stop
a bullet by inserting a thick novel by Hardy
or a Bible into a breast pocket
sited over the heart, paradoxically making the left
the forward-going shoulder
as they scrambled over the top of the ditch.

Somehow the bullets hit every limb and quadrant
outside the intended target as if deflected in flight
or else tore through the cardboard covers
of too-thin books
written off by officer-poets dying young
along with their friends.
The soldiers didn't know how it took
at least 350 pages for a novel to stop a bullet,
a fact finally established by taking modern books
to the firing range and loading the pistol
with bespoke bullets.
                          Why make tests in the day
of the Kevlar vest covering both sides of the chest?
Guilt over the old war still powers curiosity:
it was fought with magnificent stupidity,
soldiers charging in defenseless ranks,
poison gas, soft bodies and simple rifles run down
by automatic weapons and impervious tanks.

And a bloody reminder of the streets outside our windows.

SEARCHING

These are the Middle Ages
We are half way there

And back—
Listen to the keening voices
The cries of infants
Searching for their bodies

Asking their executioners
To stop waving axes like flags
As if any spirits might listen
To prayers woven in hate.

These are the Middle Ages
Before the printing press arrives
And electricity
Before antibiotics and sanitation
When the Devil ruled with torches

And nothing like humility had been invented
By the young and crawling—
No science or enlightenment
No means of communication
No perspective drawn in the dark.

We are still young and crawling.

After Some Sayings By Rabbi Earl Grollman

Death has come out of the closet, says the rabbi
                It has tentatively come for me
that walnut-sized male organ biting at my urethra
                has reminded me of my mortality
as if I could ever forget.

Grief is the price we pay for love, says the rabbi
                and I have loved too much and too many.
My trouble began with bronze-colored Yanka
                who smelled of cocoa butter oils on Brighton Beach
and cigarette smoke at home.

Living is the leading cause of death, says the rabbi
                and she was dear to me,
the only one of four grandparents to survive the war,
                she who made pancakes with jelly and fried potatoes
just for me and my useless polio leg.

I was at camp when she died and they never told me
                until I came home,
the immorality of mortality, the rabbi said
                who wasn't allowed to attend his grandmother's funeral
either. This was supposed to help me,

the subject of their whispered conversations when
                children weren't exposed to death or sex or the Holocaust.
The truth was like a circumcision
                painless and forgotten.

THE LAST JEW IN KABUL

When Zebulon Simentov, the last Jew in Afghanistan,
　　　left at sixty-two everyone was glad to be rid of him.
He turned out the lights and closed the door of the last synagogue
　　　where he once lived with Isaak Levi himself, the next to last Jew.

The last Jew in Kabul owned a kebab shop, kept kosher
　　　and prayed in Hebrew. He liked whiskey, kept a pet partridge
and charged reporters exorbitant fees for interviews.
　　　The last Persian Jew was portly and always hated the next to last Jew.

The next to last Jew in Kabul also slept in the synagogue but
　　　when Isaak died at eighty in 2005, Simentov was glad to be rid of him
even if no one was left to speak to. His wife and children had left him
　　　long ago; they fled to Israel, waiting twenty years in hope for a *get*.

The Taliban, who stole the Torah scrolls from the Ark
　　　in the synagogue and blew up the giant Buddhas of Bamiyan in 2001,
arrested the last two Jews of Kabul and beat them together
　　　but their endless bickering forced the prison guards to kick them out.

The last Jew in Afghanistan escaped from Kabul on the last bus
　　　three weeks after the Americans left; and out of desperation
twenty-nine neighborhood women and children got on the same bus
　　　as Simentov—the last Jew easier to bear when going or gone.

But the living sing the name of the last Jew in Kabul at bar mitzvahs
　　　and weddings; *Simen tov* means may it be a good omen in Hebrew.

THE LIST

Deserted by everything but memory,
    the old soldier sits in a nursing home making lists
of how they sent a teen-ager towards gunfire,
    his painful hands snipping at history like a leaf cutter

out on a branch. He tries to recall every place he was sent to
    from induction to training, from boot camp to battle zone.
His niece lends me the list. Her Uncle Max began

at Fort MacArthur in San Pedro, Camp Crowder in Neosho
    and Athens, Georgia, where he's taught to obey grunts
who never saw a Jew before. Six months of training
    in Cape Cod and Fort Dix before his embarkation;

it's 1943 when they take him away
    on the seventh day of February. *The Florence Nightingale*
goes from Fleuris to Chanzy and back to Oran.
    Max thinks he'll be as free as the ocean but the list becomes

a months-long march. By May he's in Morocco,
    readying to invade the Italian provinces of Germany:
Paestum and Battipaglia in September,
    Montella, Avellino, Maddaloni, and Caiazzo in October,

Dragoni and Fontegreca in November, marching up and down
    the spine of a country miraculously shaped like his boot.
Then comes the bloody push to Anzio in January of 1944:
    Frattamaggiore, Bagnoli, and Nettuno, their musical names

attached to ruined vineyards and stained-glass windows
    blown out in local churches. Seven historic towns in June alone:
comunes Ferriere, Velletri, Ciampino and Rome, mostly by foot,
    Santa Marinella, Bagnoli and Naples before August,

then it's on to Corsica and the invasion of France.
    At the one third point I'm too tired to look at the rest
of his "itinerary." None of us will ever see this much of the world
    this fast nor know it like he does.

I'll spare you August's six towns, the eleven in September,
    and Alsace in November, much of it made in trucks.
We're rolling with Max now, from Mannheim to Mosbach,
    to Öhringen and Welzheim, and five more towns in May,

before he enters Garmisch, the site he reminds us of the 1936
    Winter Olympics, writing "unconditional surrender"
in an almost final note as the Sixth Army Group faces down
    German troops. Austria's the eightieth tourist-stop on his tour

and Dachau the eighty-fifth, which he labels, as if we didn't know
    "[the] site of [a] notorious concentration camp."
He doesn't say what he felt but we all take a breath
    as the list unwinds in its jaunty escape to Friedlos, Le Havre

and Southampton's docks, where he ships out to New York
    on the *Queen Elizabeth*. Discharged nine days after landfall
Max ends the list on the twenty-seventh of September.
    An ordinary man, in the photos I've seen, definitely not

a Homeric hero. Born in the Bronx to Russian immigrants,
    he's half a head shorter than his wife. In other snaps
he rides a pony and wears a natty pocket square like a gentleman.
    Whether shaking hands, holding a trophy or selling liquor

Max smiles at the camera and still looks pretty well at ninety.
  As I've said, you might think he's just an ordinary man,
not that we have many of those anymore. He goes to services now,
  stumbling over the Hebrew, praying the best he can.

And when a place comes back to him, adds it to the list.

The Vanished World Of Iryna Ambramov

—May 3, 2022

In Bucha, where flowers grow fat on the graves
        and bricks and bent metal fill up the street,
young wives lose their lovers to bullets and thieves

while mothers go searching in morgues for the brave—
        four hundred sons cut down like wheat—
the flowers in March growing fat on the graves.

When hand grenades burn her house to the staves
        driving out Oleh like a cow in the street
Iryna must lose him to cutthroats and thieves.

In slippers and a bath robe missing a sleeve
        she runs out to save him knocked off his feet
in a town where the flowers shall grow fat on his grave.

One shot from behind opens his skull like a cave.
        She presses his ears spurting blood on the street
where wives lose their lovers to bullets and thieves.

In Bucha, when flowers grow fat on the graves,
        and bricks and bent metal fill up the street,
Iryna begs a soldier for death: *kill me and my cat* she raves,
        but the gun goes click and laughter roils the street.

THE SAME IS ALWAYS NOW

In the train stations and subway tunnels death flies above you.
        It's the same death on the same wings as it was before
many Springs ago, whether you were Ukrainian or a Jew.

Your feet touch the cold cement where naked bodies are stacked
        with missing fingers and limbs because the bombs drop
on the same houses and tear them off, *the same is always now.*

In place of Germans goose-stepping, Russians march with legs
        extended out of Nazi posters, heads rattling in their helmets;
they are running out of gas and bullets, even Russian bread.

Nearing Passover the current pharaoh sees the Angel of Death
        fly above his head, above the road from Moscow to Kyiv
and its geologic scar, Babi Yar, where they burnt our bodies.

The same sirens blare and children fall like silent snow;
        for some who were children here before, it's now and then:
death comes flying and life ends, always the hardest lesson.

Augenblick Is German For An Instant

Too long a word to describe so brief a time,
perfect enough to mirror one perfect lie,
recently voted the fourth most beautiful word
in the German language, it means a moment

and spoken sounds like the blink of an eye.

How lovely the recentness of an instant seems
to them, the romance of the immediate,
the thrill of what's almost gone before it arrives,
all this and more precisely incised

in a single word like heartworm in a muscle
when every beat might mean an ending
and all of existence merely a glimpse that vanishes
to that universal eye whose light has failed us.

After The Surfside Tower Collapse—June 24, 2021

Six days after
Twelve floors fell
Onto the spalled walls
Of a garage
A few wallets survive
With photos of
An elderly neighbor's child
Or a long-gone widower's wife.

Rescuers dig at
The bottom level
Atop the grim pile
Of detritus
And broken concrete
Tunneling in dust and fumes
Not daring to miss
A small hand waving
A young boy's cry
Or the whistle of gas
Before exploding bits
Of rusted rebar
Rain down,
His young life clinging to the sky
His only hope in words—
Don't leave me here
Neither dead nor alive
But lonely for life.

EVOLUTION & THE SURGEON

In my childhood the red and blue litmus papers
Defined a binary world of acid and base,
And a droplet of diatomaceous earths—
Beneath my lenses a multiplicity of lives.

I often watched a microscopic aggregation
Of unshelled atoms swim denuded before my eyes
Like half-naked bodies on the sands of Brighton Beach;
How crowded and lonely they seemed

These miniature specimens of eons past,
Scooped up and strained by cetacean hunters
Through forests of baleen on musical tongues.
It felt wonderful being a rightful descendant

Or less the predicate of what evolved in a godless dream,
Neither whale nor paramecium but a wielder of knives.

In The O.R.

Under the scope all is bright and cheery;
it's time for Mozart not Blossom Dearie.
A man with an uneven tan is on the table;
we want him to get up if he is able.

I live in a perfect pool of illumination
and flick my tools from here to there,
tracing nerves as fine as hairs—
glistered with spinal fluid and irrigation

clear as tears. Melodrama and risk
return in a mix of pride and shame.
Decades after his brain tumor did its worst
not much was saved, not even his name.

I guess it's the challenge of death I miss
waking from the horror in cautious bliss.

AUTOPSY

Meaning to see yourself or see for yourself,
To look within others or in the mirror,
As if Vesalius could dissect his own heart
And brain or any other vital part
Bequeathed by his father or mother.

If neither body nor brain has a devil's sense
Of where the cupboard of poisons is kept
Or why we brew them in darkness and when,
How can a scalpel uncover the answer?

Forensic Book Report

Somewhat short and undernourished,
this cadaver bears a partial set
of fingerprints from his right hand
and fragments of DNA from his left.
The spine's slightly bent and torn
from age and over-reading.
On the end-papers
occasional blood stains make an appearance
and a few pages stick together
where the author drew the ichor out.
Some edges were never properly cut,
the rest mildly bumped.
Library stamps and dates indicate
a low level of interest as do
rare pencil-marked exclamations in the margins.
There's a single corner fold on page 105,
when she drew a breath of self-recognition
and placed a dry flower before coming to its end.

CATECHISM

—*I wish my ignorance were more complete*, Robert Hass

Only the Sephardic eat rice at Passover
only Christian children believe He will come.

Messiah has walked out of the Garden
and into the slum.

Faith needs a purpose
like a Buddhist needs a bowl

each drop of rain a psalm
or a gift from a stranger.

Here is Abraham's tent, its four sides lifted open
at the crossroads

to all who believe in a single One.
And here I am perplexed

at the crowd spying on me in the mirror
watching me watching them.

The Coup

When the generals dress in suits and ties
they will bear titles
like delegate and representative of the people.
They will feed the widow
and bury the child.
Each spring the garden will grow the same apple
passing it from tree to tree.
The catamount will sing with the strongest,
the worker in his mirror, the police in their cars.
My tulip poplars will lose their blossoms at the start of Spring.

The generals will make peace with our enemies
and war with our friends.
They will make gods of themselves
and slaves of their subjects.
They will smile in the afternoon
and frown at midnight.
They will pass laws for others but not for themselves.
They will still look like the sort of Boy Scout
who helps an old lady cross a street against her will.

They always tell us attendance is voluntary
but don't you ever fail to come to the meetings.

APOCALYPSE

The hollow head
The head hollow
Hollow is the head
How hollow is the head?
How hollow the head is
It is very hollow
The hollow head is hallow
So hollow is the head
That it is hallow
Hallowed be the head hollow
Hallowed be the hollowed head
A hallowed head is hollow
It must follow
That the dead head is hallowed
A dead head is hollow
A hollow head is hallowed
The dead's head is hallowed
In death the head is hallowed
The dead death's head is hallowed
The hollow head of death is hallow
Hallowed be this hollowed head
What death the hollow head?
How came this head now hallowed?
A shallow death to the hollow head
The hallowed head died a shallow death
So shallow the hollow of hallowed head
So shallow the hollowed head
In a shallow hollow the head's death
In death a shallow hollow
All death in a shallow hollow
How shallow the hallowed death
How shallow the hollow
How dead.

PASS-OVER

The innocents torn to bits
lay scattered in David's city
like crumbs of unleavened bread.

This time the Angel of Death
did not pass our doors but struck us
with a bomb strapped to his chest
and a smile as old as Egypt.

I want to give him some advice—
it's better to lose the land
than to end up a beast in heaven
but no one is listening now.

Better to heed Jonah's example
I say, similarly grieved,
who wished a death from bitterness
God refused to grant.

We both may need what Kafka meant
an axe to crack
the frozen sea within us.

Poem After A Line By Henri Cole

Scrubbing off the past that cannot be scrubbed off
Is exhausting:

> All those songs and marches
>
> The prayers and curses
>
> The paying of dues
>
> And ultimately the lying

All make me tired and short of breath
Like swimming against a tidal wave in a quiet harbor
Or getting a kite out of a tree. Or a cat.

My hands are rough from making peace in my own head,
Sore and red from making sensible arguments agree:

> Each side of me gets one ear
>
> One arm, one leg and one eye
>
> But I have only one mouth
>
> Therefore, I must decide

Whether I will fly with the birds
Or scurry with the mammals
Whether I am a bat or merely batty.

All the world is in an amiable conspiracy
I am the one who is up in the tree.

III
BODY & BRAIN

An artist only needs a good idea and too little time—
Leonard Bernstein

ASCRIPTIVE

—Walter Charleton, 1650

Last used perhaps by a homeopath
who tried curing wounds with magnets,
ascriptive is almost invisible in the OED
and banned from *Chambers Dictionary*.

A word my computers always erase
gave way to ascribed in the 17th century
until an essay in yesterday's *Times*
caught me into flipping the script:

Ascriptive might have meant
hand printing in block letters
without using a more elegant script

Or improvisation while acting
after brief instruction on a stage
in the absence of text;

Or else an archaic system
England used to pay for groceries
in place of real money during a war;

Or the taking of medications
illegally
without a doctor's prescription;

Or something we badly need
in opposition to our politics—

Anything but imputation:
a seeing without thinking
of skin color
the accent of their voice
gender or class
or the flag they are waving

A script without being.

AT THE UNIVERSAL

He is working behind me.
From where I tread in the gym
I can see him in the mirror
an old man holding vertically
a plastic body-blade
first in the right and then the left fist;
its edge looks like a magician's wand
with the length of a hunting bow.

Almost weightless the wand's movement
exercises the triangular latissimus muscles
running towards each shoulder from his spine
and vibrates back and forth
inscribing a soundless harp in the air.

How weak does an old man have to be
for his muscles to respond in this way?
Perhaps he is freeing his joints
from arthritis, made worse by age
or a fall.
Perhaps he's simply enchanted
by that which cannot be measured—
the pleasure of moving anything alive
like an electron in the tail of a comet.

MISSING THE SUPERFLUOUS

It's taken the music out of the air,
the gym out of the muscle,
the drink out of the bar,
and grandchildren out of the state
we live in.
Self-entertainment has died.
An old lady asks on the radio
have you ever tried to play pinochle
six feet apart, a riddle worthy of Pythagoras.
She's noticed how the blondes
in her retirement home
sport roots as gray as the brunettes,
how everyone's hair has curled up
like a dry mop.
They're all waiting for Phase 3
and permission to breathe without a mask.
Too old to save,
the straps have come off my sense of time
and all the clocks have turned to confetti.

Outside In My Underwear

Sitting outside in my underwear
I watch the hot blue-gray sky
darken with clouds,
my eyes searching out a visitation
of small white butterflies
amid the slow chase of a blinking
firefly, its indecisive light aping
my mood. My wife's just left
crazed by cabin fever,
she's desperate for an evening run
on the cracked sidewalk cement
of neighborhood blocks.
The heat has silenced the crickets,
gone well beyond their thermal
sweet spot, as steamed leaves fall
like small parachutes
from the heights of tulip poplars,
gently smacking my face and calves,
loosened by an itinerant breeze.
A lone red deer mincingly strolls
the boundary line between our yard
and the house next door,
each of her halting steps cautioned
by the noise of forced laughter
entertaining their guests like ghosts.

POOL POEM [1]: A DAISY CHAIN OF POOLS

Swimming in Wendy's pool next door I start each lap
below the white blooms of a Crape Myrtle and end
where orange daylilies lie shadowed
by a brown Magnolia.
After the seventeen-year cicadas re-enter the ground
and the dry shells of their exoskeletons
turn to powder, summer arrives a bit early
with memories of summers past.

At six, an unlucky boy in Bensonhurst swims
in a public pool filled with polio virions
and becomes stuck in bed for six months or more.
At seven or eight my parents took my shriveled leg
by overnight train to Miami where I paddle for a week
heated by the summer sun. At an Art Deco Hotel
dressed with porthole windows, I hold my breath
for the first time and Father kicks me a soccer ball
at the edge of the ocean. By nine or ten
I go swimming in Lake George with a first girl,
"cousin" Ruthie, the daughter of Dad's best friend,
and the lake remains so still it feels like a pool
but for the guppies swarming between our legs.

I leave for school in Boston at sixteen
and my folks move to a house in Old Saybrook
with a fenced-in pool we hardly use.
I'd read *The Swimmer* by Cheever by then
and seen the movie in which Burt Lancaster swims
eight miles from home in Connecticut, one backyard pool
after another and loses his mind. Polio too

is that kind of gift, it keeps on giving. This year
I swim across the alley from one epidemic to the next,
needing to loosen my piriformis because a shortened left leg
and pelvic tilt are giving me sciatic pain.
Despite not having a pool of my own the circle seems closed.

Pool Poem [4]: Coda

The pool ripples like a poem, a collage of botanicals
and zoology, of isolation and nostalgia.
To know our history is to know our future;
when the dense foliage interlaces above my head,
even the sky disappears. I came here to go.

I remember the boy who slept in my childhood bed
how neoprene dinosaurs roared on the sheets
how the radio bled the singing world into his ears.
Everything was voiced, every object spoke to me.

Soon after the seventeen-year-cicadas
drill into the ground and before I'm set to leave go
the water turns cold, the mating dragonflies
with blue tuxedoed bellies fall out of the sky,
the wasps disappear and the Monarchs fly off to Mexico.
All that remains is an inflatable pink flamingo
smiling on the concrete skirt of the pool.

Mostly steering a straight course through the water,
I'm relieved to spy the white nipple in the shallow end
that once fed the pool's fountain;
I close my goggled eyes and feel my body aiming
at its target, the GPS in my head like slag iron.

Bittersweet

O the bargains I struck
On the nights before surgery
Agreed:
The gain of more useful life
At the possible cost
Of a palsied arm or clumsy speech,
The rescue of nerves that see
At a possible loss of
Olfactory memory;
The end of pain in a bruised back
For a weakened limb.
All these and more
Acceptable to me
Before our roles and chances
exchanged
From doer to done upon
And a tumor removed
From beneath my bladder.

I was struck then with the smell
Of uric acid everywhere,
Slapped with the constant wet
Of drip on my leg
And worse
The loss of intimacy.

From that first night
She became as distant as the moon
And life took on a new mealy taste
The apple had turned bittersweet.

Not Like A Poem

Life is and is not like a poem.
The poem enters a room with variable dimensions
And all at once I feel it sway.
My feet enter a room and its colors are always the same.

A line comes dressed with the surprise of sudden stops
And redresses itself with every turn it makes into the next;
There is no dirty laundry hanging on the line.
A day without lines is a day filled with boredom.

An average line escapes like a melodic flute or trombone
Towards the back of an orchestra;
In my everyday world it's the only instrument I play.
I pay out the line as the poem nears its dock.

A poem has a theory of movement and each movement a sign;
A life has more movements and hopes for more time.

ULTIMATE DISAPPOINTMENT—
after Joseph Roth's Preface to *The Wandering Jews* (1937)

In our short lives, shorter than the life of the elephant,
The crocodile, and the crow, even the parrot,
There's too little time to recognize the face in the mirror,
The voice on the phone, the voice in the poem.

I'm estranged from myself and all the earth.
At least I know it, I am a Jew, but you, who are you
And which one of me is speaking to you?
Time has eliminated place, erased any possible home.

That will come as packed dirt sooner than you expect.
In the time of the Einsatzgruppen no one went alone.
Nothing gets done in a grave, no books or video or gin;
No room to stretch our arms. We finish as a concept,

An idea, if lucky, a memory whispered during Yahrzeit.
Hoping for heaven or hell when all God says "this is it."

BLUE SMOKE INSIDE MY HEAD
(On Looking at My MRI)

Today I saw a blue jay land on a backyard poplar
While I puffed away on a Parejo from Havana
Its blue smoke rising inside my head
Behind my eyes and along my spinal cord
Bristling like a tree or worn-out toilet brush
In Baltimore.
                    This season I'm covered in blue—
My mouth, my throat, my unhappy mood dressed
In the world's favorite color by actual vote,
Coiling and uncoiling like a blue racer's spawn
As my brain's cyanotype fills with musical notes.

This year there was no fire just the smoke
It seemed to extinguish every hope; I know
The ancient Greeks had no word for the color blue,
See Homer's wine-dark sea and rosy-fingered dawn.

THE FIRE INSIDE YOUR HEAD
(Looking at a Colorized MRI of Your Brain)

Here lies consciousness in the brain stem, its power plant
of energetic fibers traveling up towards the corpus callosum
of a person captured in a moment of wakefulness spread
to the right and left brains, near the blushing red fingerprint
of a small guided missile computer, the cerebellum tilted out
of its bony basement, and everywhere else invisible energy
washed in the blue sulci between red-green forests
of curving cortex, where crystalline fluid bathes the gyri
clean of exfoliated toxins and metabolic spillage.

On our left the heavy frontal lobes hang facing down as if
the head's engaged in an acrobatic flip, its owner tumbling
on a floor mat or reaching for the lowermost bar
in a qualifying gymnastic stunt. Or else it's your own head bent
to a research bench or at a writer's desk in a concentrated instant
of thought worrying over an equation or rhythmic sentence.
Either way we all can share a creaturely pride in looking
at such a normal scan digitally painted with colorful flames
to highlight the machine's mysterious activity.

GRATITUDE

Thank God for science, for the two eyes,
Two hands and two ears
That investigate the world
For the brain that invents its own world
For the feet that know when to turn away
For the heart that knows when to pray
For the nose that goes just ahead of us
And the generations who went before
For the gift of DNA, in all its stability
And mutability
For the love of charm and spore
Invisible neutrino and weighty quark
The animals who left the ark
And that blessed wedge between light and dark.

A Sonnet Plus One About The Brain

Within the brain a thought is a function of time, $f(t)$,
and a diffident occupier of space, $f(x)$;
it moves from place to place, $x(t)$, on a whim
in an attempt at discovery (S = Surprise).

The summary of places it's been, $\Sigma(x_0 \ldots x_n)$
is a circuit and its content a memory, $M(x)$
or Memorex, with the shape of a sail
depending on wind (W) and trim.

The wind is a type of energy (E) or metaphor
blowing through the brain with a passion and force
as an emblem of the century $F(c)$ in which it lives
even if its breath blows on the embers
of a richer previous age $F(c-1)$. Therefore

any fashionable thought is proportional to the ratio
$F(c)$ divided by $F(c-1)$ and anything goes.

IV

EKPHRASIS

....my imagination started to work, had begun to paint.
—Proust: *Remembrance of Things Past*, vol.7, p.3366

Painting is silent poetry and poetry is painting with the gift of speech
—*Simonides of Ceos* (b.556 BCE)

OBJECTS REMOVED FOR STUDY

Like the sign in every museum says
in this glass case or on that wall
something has disappeared
only temporarily we hope
if nothing should change in our memory.

Meaning no adjectival nouns are missing here
just the time and energy of presence
as it stands in a corner or hangs on a wall
and says *look at me*
for beauty or understanding
like a person might
such artworks being as needy of care as we are
but rarely as vocal
unless a playable violin or cello
by Strad or Guarneri.

As time moves towards us
how much do we really miss one of several stones
in a jewelry vitrine
or a single Achaean cup from a crowded wing
devoted to Ancient Art?

We may or may not be brought to tears
by the loss of a small Dutch portrait
rendered on a copper medallion
or worse the loan of a favorite Rembrandt
and the seemingly sudden absence of a Vermeer
a cause certain of heartache or frustration.

Why isn't it here we ask ourselves
and do we remember who stood at our side
as when we last shared the experience?
Are they still alive or in need of repair?
Perhaps that will come later when we too are gone
and no one has hung a sign for us.

Two Modern Architects

What's this strange attraction I've got for architects
      found dead or dying in the street?
First there was Gaudi, hit by a tram in Barcelona,
      his beard dusted with cracked bottles and broken plates,
three days laying in a hospital unknown
      before they knew to bury him below his Sagrada Familia,
and now Louis Kahn, his coal-scarred face
      found sea-blue in Penn Station, too poor to get on
or off his train, just back from Bangladesh
      and exhausted by keeping three separate households
going in suburban Philadelphia—a feat
      of almost Palladian symmetry—one wife and two women
of the other kind who made one child per house.
      What a gift to be famous and poor (almost poet-like)
chained to lintel and architrave,
      he who never erected a tall spire to his own ambition,
using vaulted roofs only, ever a specialist in the design
      of light-filled tombs and his own doubt-built grave.

A DREAM OF MORDEN TOWER

There are few places more romantic than a graveyard
        where one can feel the warm cloak of ghosts,
like the emanations of Yeats congealing at Ballylee,
        that square fifteenth century Thoor I've never seen,
when he was at home spying on the swans at Coole.
        Or stepping inside the round Martello tower
at Sandycove might be just as good,
        where Joyce spent a week in 1904, years before
Stately, plump Buck Mulligan voyaged down its steps
        with a bowl of lather in which mirror and razor lay crossed,
like those island nations on either side of the Irish Sea,
        that blue-green line on the map of violence and poetry.

My newest miss was the drum-shaped Morden Tower
        in Newcastle on Tyne, one of five survivors standing
from the thirteenth century in the old medieval wall.
        Panic and distress arrived in me learning of this too late
a moment before I gave a reading at the university,
        a few sophists of certainty sitting in front,
not one with the courtesy to mention the old literary pipe
        or issue me a pass to leave off the dinner and tour
the ancient archeology of the site
        rescued at last by battalions of poets in 1964,
the town having blown much of its history on priests
        and guilds of glaziers, plumbers, and goldsmiths.

These mythic towers encase the epidemiology of poetry
        in which I remain immiserated and a touch insane,
supposing never to walk in Newcastle again,
        never to share the residual breath of its elder voices
taking their own deep dive in a deep green sea,
        or feel my body tingle at a Whitmanian frequency.

If only I had seen the Morden Tower bit by lightning,
        sparking the sky like a volcano on Mordor,
it might have lit something universal in me
        exploding the bias of personal history, clearing away
the fumes of Brooklyn, Boston and Baltimore.

And yet childhood nights held a similar waking dream,
        my body afloat on the ceiling, freed of shackles and bed,
free of the polio leg that had kept me grounded by day,
        when the spirit of poetry first descended on me
and a paralysis of sort left my brain.

BUILT TO BE MUTE, THE PAUSE

That space between the words
makes the rhythm on which they dance
line to line

The silent abstract paintings on the walls
speaking within us
with self-reflection

Even humble objects—
the brass bell cast without a clapper
planted in the earth to make the crops grow
its empty slits like eyes
(*dotaku*)
the wound of silence after their maker
is gone

If wise we pause heavily
in the business of life
a brief rest from the mercenary

Like that meditative space for cloistered monks
pausing in the breath of their psalms
or the musicians who approach complete silence:
a mute in the mouth of a horn

Debussy's auratic ineffable sounds
between the notes
and Miles building music out of those he didn't play.

THE ORIGINAL GLIMPSER

He wasn't a poet but a painter. Friends called him Bill,
      his critics de Kooning; I didn't know him
and never got to visit the house on Long Island.
      Since I and my generation lived with his art
all our lives I will call him Bill. That is to say
      what I gleaned of his character was only from paintings
and hundreds of thousands of words on blank pages.
      Glimpsing gave Bill an idea how representation
and abstraction really worked, one and the same.
      There's a famous story almost no one knows
about Bill's kindness standing next to a guy
      who didn't know it was him in the museum.
The man gently asked if he should feel ashamed
      to see real things like breasts and buttocks
or even women's faces in such violent slashes of paint.
      Bill's reply was a kind of intellectual permission,
a blessing or benediction I often use in class:
      there's nothing so abstract it doesn't have a resemblance.
He felt you have to change in order to remain the same
      and practiced slipping out from the upright world.
Daily he would fall at odd angles, stealing a quick look
      for getting to reality "on the beam." After almost a century
of drowning in drink, Bill was more than a bit demented
      but kept making art to the end, re-inventing his name
as "slipping glimpser." Bill's countryman van Gogh
      was deep in his bones when he stowed away
on a New York bound freighter in 1926.
      What they glimpsed for seconds we stare at for hours.

THE TORCH OF ENTHUSIASM
—R. Middleman (1935-2021)

Raoul died last night
who could talk faster than a Bay oyster
sliding down your gullet.

I often drowned in his enthusiasm
for art and philosophy,
even at the gym,
spittle shooting from his mouth.

He remembers his first studio
above the strip clubs on The Block
and ten thousand canvases left in storage
with nowhere else to go.

Our two brains were always at war.
He never made me a gift
though I spent a day sitting for him
and wrote a poem I never put in a book.

He knew I hated his portrait of me
painted with his usual energy—
it made me look like an evil dwarf.

I once wrote an article about him
but he never thanked me.
Kings don't thank their subjects.

JO IN THE LIGHT
—after Edward Hopper's Woman in the Sun, 1961

While Bonnard always painted his wife
as a young girl, an orange memory in a tub,
Hopper presents his as grim and naked
edging out of life.

In the last picture, she watches
the sun set through an unseen window.
She holds an unlit cigarette,
her eye downcast.
There's nothing erotic about the pose.

Flat and thin, she is soaked
in a rectangle of light
cut by the twin shadows of her legs.
The geometry continues
in the parallel shape of an unmade bed.

Pressed against the brown frame
Jo cues us by its narrowness
that the heat of late Impressionism has sped
into the cold abstraction of American Realism.

Hopper's Rooms By The Sea (1951)

He lived long enough to try it,
a room without an isolated figure
not even Jo
no usher at the movies
no frumpy furniture
or New York mansard roofs
or any other urban clue,
an imaginary space in which
diagonal sunlight enters knife-like
slices through a blue-gray wall
until his interior view floats out
towards the horizon
of sea and sky
leaving its door wide open—
an empty room
a room someone unseen has left
or was it his soul
jumping over the threshold
and into the ocean
tired of reality.

BAR TALK / BARTOK

There are things you can't say or do now
in the wrong environment or else
friendship may end at the door
after you blow a jar or two
of Talisker Ten
and the brown gray fur of your coat
gets hung as you implore a corner
to shake the rain from your bumble shoot
with one foot on the rail of the bar
and the other planted on its floor
just before the final word of your bar talk
makes a claim of cultural superiority
and planting your face softly breaks
your nose on the fist of gravity,
a certain clarity comes.
No one shares your interests any more—
you can catch a cold before his name
rings a bell in this neon emporium.
Bartok he says, *Bela Bartok, I can't say
if I recall*; we were born after he died
and nothing in New York lasts that long.

The Difference Example Makes

You don't have to take my word for it,
interrogate Rilke's eyeless torso of Apollo
or ask Jim Wright lazily a-swing on his farm
in Duffy's hammock, feeling his future sting.

Hour after hour of writing poems they tell me
can be all or nothing, even those of our master
Yeats, nothing happens beyond futile beauty
as Auden wrote in mourning our greatest great.

Why waste the hours putting words to paper
if limning a portrait with paint is often quicker
or composing music that much richer,
our opinions hidden and proof against burning?

Stevens and Williams also lived outside their art
examples of difference that gave me heart.

Building A Prize-Winner

Alter their Meanings the words that might trigger
(See Fascist and Communist)
Don't study History
Concentrate on Typography
Use Spaces and capitals between Persons   and People
Employ Erasures and Blank lines
███████████████
When Necessary
Be Gay but not too Happy
Be Young and not any Older
Stay Woke   and never Drowsy
Explore the Present and Past   in the present Tense
Use Greek terms found in a Dictionary
Without explanation or Notes
Don't use Rhyme or Alliteration
Or Punctuation
Cancel something or anyone bigger than a Stamp
Act Correct but not Right
Go Left or be Left behind
Feel sad and angry about Yourself
Your Country and the World
Don't make Fun of anything or anyone
Don't use Puns or humor or anything Off-color
No laughter or Sarcasm
Only Hit at Targets pre-approved on Social Platforms
Attack every Religion and The Enlightenment
Shakespeare and Baudelaire
Shun Movies from the Thirties
Picture books from the Fifties
Novels like *Brave New World* and *1984*
Science and Statistics
Evolution and Black Holes
Make Prose look like Verse and Poems like Prose
Avoid iambic Pentameter and French whenever possible
The period at The End is optional (.)

Painted Lions Catch On Fire

The bullshit of surrealism goes back and forth
From meaning to no meaning
And back again
From decade to decade like the seventeen-year cicadas
Like the child you've raised against its will
Asleep in your house for the last time
Between going off to college and those scholastic lies
You rejected decades ago at the same age
As if words were a science and not a guess:

Why do we live in a museum my daughter asks
Why do all your patients die my son quizzes?

The manes of finely painted lions catch on fire
The sun swallows the earth the sun later swallowed
By a black hole where God does not throw dice
A prediction an old man made against his will
The Second Coming or a corporate meeting
On an operating room table
A soundless umbrella and a sewing machine
A man with a bowler hat and a cane
Immobile floating in the sky forever.

REFLECTIVE SONNET

The space that opens is the space that closes.
Looking East I no longer can see the West.
My arms feel light when I'm done lifting heavy.
In the midst of sadness the soul takes flight.
Who are you to tell me how I must live.
When filled with love I am done with envy.
In the fullness of age I get steadily younger.
In the midst of weakness I feel much stronger.
In the onrushing crowd is the onset of lonely.
In thrall to splendor I'm struck with sadness.
Giving in to knowledge I'm filled with humility.
Knowing more and more I am learning less.
In every ending there's a new beginning.
In the center of certainty there's only a guess.

V
IN THE TWILIGHT

How far away the stars seem, and how far
Is our first kiss, and ah, how old my heart!

—W. B. Yeats, *Ephemera* (1884)

QUARRELING, FOR US, WAS A KIND OF INTIMACY

—John Banville

Is this not the case for all couples? We debate and sabotage the other
        he or she who most resembles ourselves or the mother or brother;
we exclaim *fuck off* as if it were really goodbye and not a verbal kiss.

After so many years we two are falcons flying alone together,
        enemy combatants or invaders of this house, like wishful revenants
who miss the magic of their original sin, the trick that sticks like glue.

You are licking postage stamps and cutting out coupons of bliss,
        those sticky papers of domestic gifts, an electronic cuckoo clock,
an automatic garbage disposal, the screw that squeezes the orange.

Who made me king, who crowned you queen, who gave a thought
        to a new beginning? We were the cowards who ran with the crowd
like bulls in the street, because we were afraid of our feelings.

And now we are old, five decades on, and hardly as wise as stumps,
        we seek what meaning means beyond the hump, beyond the thinking
and after dinner with a wine or two and the inevitable drowsy slump
        I take your hand in mine and argue for love and a new beginning.

Mosquito Erotica

In our warm September back-yard the mosquitoes come
one by one, a single bite at a time,
the inside thigh and the base of the thumb
favorite targets.
They itch, they swell but I rarely run
from what my wife finds unbearable—
humming inside with her Cuba Libre, coke and rum.
I cheer her with an old bromide, how sweet is her blood.

The scientist in me knows it's not just blood,
the chief attractants being warmth and carbon dioxide,
the *je ne sais quoi* of a body's ineffable charm
those subtle smells of hidden warmth and wet enticing
the pheromone and insecticide of my come.

Sixty-five years on I'm surprised to discover
our evolutionary link, a nosy mosquito without wings.

In This House

The days grew longer—
They'd lost their natural rhythm
And melody
And you knew you were growing older,
Sleeping more and getting less rest
While forgetting the lyrics
To song after song.

You tried hard to remember
But at the end of the day
They were gone,
Those little bits of you
Now belonged to a stranger
You'd met somewhere else
And no longer knew.

CONVERGENCE OF THE DEAD
—Hoffman, Lux, Allen, Wilbur & Hall

Though these revenants may arrive any time they wish,
      all must come to my overcrowded meeting place—
fortunate to miss the pandemic,
      the recession and the riots, all of which supplanted
(but not for me)—the sorrow of their passing.

They come in the order of their leaving,
      heroes and friends, and proponents of good living
gentle lives of fierce loving and kind witness.

Hoffman is the first; I can hear the crepitation in his lungs
      moist with salt water from constant weeping for his wife
and behind him the spectral tribes immortalized in his verse.
      Look who's come, Dan exclaims topping a bourbon for Tom
with a maraschino cherry, his favorite taste.

An image of veined arms and flowing hair fills my mind,
      his warm voice and smiling charm outlive the cells
that killed him too soon. Dick arrives at cocktail time,
      his Buddhist heart having crashed on Christmas day.

He bears sweet lyrics gathered from small-town signs
      and folk songs heard on cross-country summer jaunts
made in Lori's ancient Honda. I am set to wonder if
      Allen's angel shares his fear of flying?

Near the party's end we all get up in greeting Wilbur
      as he enters the room reciting a few of his perfect rhymes
in meter. All this toasting and talking tests my sense
      of reality—but Don Hall's presence off in a corner
reassures me, he's taking notes.

Moreover, the last and oldest New Englanders,

     Hall and Wilbur look pretty good for making it to eternity.

During the plague I didn't dare tell them Fenway Park

     had closed but I suspect Tom Lux (as usual) already knows.

Travesties Of Aging

I'm learning how to walk up and down my stairs again
in PT—down towards Hell with the bad left leg
up towards Heaven with the good one on the right—
the cane always poised on the same tread as the polio leg,
a synchronicity too complex for my ancient head.

This morning my prostate began its farewell tour;
a month or two from now a surgeon and his robot
will expel my swollen organ with its spots of tumor
from its complacent abode in my pelvis
where it has made almost no contribution for years.

The smallest and most useless organ in the body—
I don't know whether my wife ever felt its action
and am afraid to ask. I know this morning
I squirted a little and when he squirts I squirt.
I naturally think of him as a he or Mr. Prostate.

I fear this is just the start of my disassembly—
my gradual disappearance part by part.

A Cold Chemical Light Gives Warning

Sometimes I don't recognize what I am doing
as I am doing it amid the sly dance of consonants,
how a shy rhyme sneaks in by late morning
or why a nature the opposite of exuberance
lights up in the evening when the fireflies arrive
and the answer sits cupped in my hand,
its wistful battery going on and off
like a green navigational mark at the dock's end.

The firefly moves my concentration from the grassland
to the water watching dark pilings at the mouth of a river
approach as slowly as a silent illusion,
the mind's boat gliding past an unintended accident
and something in memory I no longer do as well
in the absence of the firefly's cold chemical light.

Aboard Sirène in the Morning

There's nothing as beautiful as a marina at dawn
the clacking of ducks
the sky clearing away
the remnants of a storm:

A silvery sky
and a breeze sun-filled
and warm
the steel halyards at rest
from beating on mast and boom
the loom of shadows withdrawing
from the wheel
in the cockpit
the city awakening too soon
like a cat in search of a meal.

The cabins in my sailboat line up
like the lenses in a telescope
the rays of the rising sun
pricking through
from back to front
finally reach into the bow
warming the V-berth
and wake me to the morning.

The tide runs low—
soon there will be
feet on the dock boards
and halyards stamping in a stronger breeze
carrying the smell of coffee
and the children asleep below
don't yet feel or know
the wonder of the world.

A Bay Fisherman's Meteorological Lesson

Good clouds flying west to east make no argument against
the planet's breath while their horsetails banner the sky.

If we meet in angry confrontation, it's an offshore front
hiding the sun and landing in a tumbling punt

with increasing frequency, gust after gust pushing too close
to jagged rocks in rising oceans I'd rather not see,

my innards twisted by vain hopes of reality.
Everything turns in its motion at once, not just our homes

but fishing boats soaked by a two-ton punch
hitting the gunnels, throwing souls and stomachs to the sky.

A pandemic of fear snaps free my gimlet eye as I await
a drop of courage to steer us safely by

having left the sea for a cozy room with pictures of calmer waves
in a rain-soaked town, a drink at my side and a cat to lea.

AT THE KEYBOARD (A KADDISH)

I've not erased the dead from my birthday alarm:
My tickler celebrates birth over death
The app on my computer nudging memory against
A future filled with the loss of friends.

In digital tombstones made of zeros and ones
Endings are ignored in favor of life's start—
Each em dash trailed by a void.
Parents recompose in my electrons, so do some poets.

Seeing their faces and hearing their voices in my head
Is one more test of meaningful existence,
All of us going on living until those remembering
Join in the army of the dead

When I suppose in a new tomorrow
Only robots will be left this side of the screen.

WHERE GUESTS ONCE SLEPT
(No.3 *from* EIGHT ROOMS FOR AN OLD HOUSE) —*for Ilene*

The most beautiful room in the house is the guest room
where she dresses and leaves piles of fresh laundry.
The walls have old prints and paintings with real faces
and on the floor wooden chairs and two towers of books.
Sunlight walks in from northern facing windows
without any squeal from the traffic rumbling outside.
Here the day neither rises nor falls on the low bed
from which my legs have trouble lifting my old body
and the house wraps you in a white cloth of silence
like a body prepared for burial, quiet and still, free
from anxiety at last. This upstairs room, almost as high
as the poplar trees outside is free of all distraction. Yet
I've not written a word in this room where once
billiard balls clanked in dark pockets and we made bets.

HARD-BOILED DICKS

—after Laura, 1944

Before we go out my wife laughs a little when she hears me mumble *hard-boiled dicks* thinking I'm thinking something dirty, like women did before the automobile, the pill and the freedom to do anyone at any time as if what had been good enough for men was just as good for them—STDs, loss of innocence, loss of pride, not waiting for that great first love in a dream of perpetual loyalty to the future. Me, I'm dreaming all the way back to the Forties and Fifties, speaking of film, and dames and gats, of a black and white celluloid world filled with shame and disgust. At this point I'm practicing my hardest Brooklyn stare while looking in the mirror and straightening my tie when I catch sight of a pimple at the side of my nose, a tense lump of pain smaller than a pill. Suddenly I'm ready to crumple from medical student's disease, afraid to squeeze lest it cause much later, an abscess in my brain's frontal lobe, almost the first thing I learned not to do in medical school and the last I hope to forget. Oh yes, lesson two back then was to stay out of the sun—nothing worse than melanoma, especially if you live at night like Dracula or I do and you must keep your skin pale and safe, like Bogey & Bacall's or Dana Andrews in that celluloid dream I've entered, that hard-boiled dick who mooned over a woman he'd never met, listening to the music play while looking at Laura's face. Now we've both gotten ready and my tie is straight; I hold my hands up like a camera, sighting my wife as she steps into the frame my fingers make.

Sonomama Or My Wife's Flowers

I stand behind her in my most natural pose,
as attentive as a Japanese farmer lost in *sonomama*,
and watch her plant dozens of "a million bells"
in every yard, lavender blue Calibrachoa
and pink stars with central white dots,
each small face possessing a single cartoon eye
sequestered in pots of red clay—
silent sentinels set at the doors front and back,
others hidden behind walls of Maryland stone.

She packs them together with cheerful pink Lantana
and almost 415 species of Lobelia
with a Petunia Wave trailing like a vine.
Her strategy confuses me, not to mention freighted
with unpronounceable Latin names
Torenia, Verbena and Vinca, joins in a crush
of blossoms like a traffic jam in every direction
on all four arms of a compass card.

No matter what they're called they look like petunias
to me, I'm a guy and city poet, and the only plants I know,
Geraniums and Impatiens, agree with my temper.
In the living kaleidoscope she's built
I would lose all direction if I were a bee.
My wife straightens and points me towards the house;
I find it easily, grateful for the signposts of roses and trees.

Earworms

When you can't get a word
or words out of your head
until it nests between the ears—
early on Sinatra singing
one more for the road
until poetry came my way—
and she said:
because death couldn't wait for me
and he said:
so long as this doth live
so long lives thee.

Before the grass overwhelms you
like a nylon blanket warming the sun
on your knees
and you feel the bloodworm
or earthworm
getting closer
to body and brain
listen to the voices asking
what creature is this in my ear
preparing the soil and grass for me
and after I might answer
it is the soil of fear
and the grass of inevitability.

THE DOCTOR WHO TREATS HIMSELF HAS A FOOL FOR A PATIENT

—Sir William Osler, 1849-1919

The first night alone I re-warmed my wife's meatloaf and made rice
    with cinnamon on top; the next dinner a roast beef sandwich with chips.
All week I ate out with friends: fried chicken, spare ribs, duck confit—
    not a single meal with anything from the ocean except oysters.
Neighbors who knew better fed me cube steak and home-fried potatoes.

I'd spent the month before leaking from my rectum and worrying over
    a tumor of the bowel or paralysis of my anal sphincter.
A day after wife and daughter left, I didn't even fart as much as the cat!
    I thought it must be my nightly martini or pizza, or probably stress,
too much tuna or purified water. As a test I stopped doing anything healthy

or politically correct. When the hips started hurting and my left leg went numb
    down to the toes I was certain my spine had narrowed at sixty or else
I had pissed a disc into my tail-bone. Four days later all symptoms had gone
    when I heard my wife at the door shouting "Honey, we're home."

New Yorkers

in memory of Roger & Lorelle Phillips

He was born right here, seven blocks from where they still live,
Lenox Hill between Park and Lex,
where his wife now lies with a scarf on her head,
to hide the fallen hairs of radiation.

She wears a boot on her foot from an accident in the park:
his wife still feisty fifty years after they wed.
My friend sits on the edge of her bed a little confused
in the looming light of facing windows.

Downstairs the incubator of his past sits,
the room of his beginning, and down the Avenue something
he'd rather not know what was coming comes
this Saturday morning when the trees turn up
their wrinkled palms to the Fall.

Cat In Quarantine

Claude loves tomato sauce on pasta
though not lasagna
unlike that fat cat in the comics.
Claude eats dry cat chow only
when he wants to.
You might say he's spoiled.
Claude loves to eat what we eat
and when we eat it:
milk from a cereal bowl,
chicken, sirloin, sometimes fish,
and popcorn only when I throw it
letting him bat it from paw to paw
as if each kernel was a field mouse
recently caught, hockey puck
or laser light
before licking the salt and crushing it
with his teeth.
Claude does not floss or use a Water pik.
He likes to lick watermelon slices.

As the months pass there are changes:
Claude no longer follows me up the stairs
but dozes instead on the kitchen island
in an especially soft circular bed
designed to avoid irritation
of his neck hairs.
Claude now prefers to stand
at the toilet bowl
in the powder room disdaining
his automated water fountain.
During a check-up at the vet
assistants fight for the privilege

of holding him for a weight check
and discover more Claude than before
from eight-point-two to ten-point-two
or twenty-five percent.
It's not all fur or fair.
The cat and his staff must go on a diet.

Dust In The Streets

My Uncle Alfred lies in New Jersey,
my parents off a highway in New London,
my stepmother in Boston.
And then there are the ashes scattered
without stones, generations of the burnt
and pillaged, all-over Europe,
those lost to memory, living in poems.

I can't sleep. At four the cat follows me
into a dark room and purrs under my left hand
as I write inscriptions for family tombs
in my lap. We're surrounded by shelved books
and tomes in piles on every side.
They lie like closed eyes
at night in the ledgers the Germans used
to settle their accounts, boxcars of fillings
and ashes. I'm out of memories and facts,
my disc-drive frozen, my dump truck empty
of dirt. The promise of America and the auto
tore our little family in different directions
geographic and otherwise as if to complete
the work of the Poles and Dutch, the Swiss
and Germans. We're like dust in the street
dressing the bright lights of Broadway.

CROSSING THE TAPE

Perhaps you too have known Durer's famous four—
Famine, Pestilence, Death and War
The woodcut of prophecy he made in Germany,
Where he was born.

Fate tried killing me twice,
At least once before I was born,
Killed every grandparent of mine with hate save one,
Drove Father and Mother into hiding
Where they fought to be safe.
I grew proud of their every escape
When we finally crossed the tape into America.

I was a boy of six when polio came dressed as Fate,
It tore my left leg right out from under me,
Taught me to read in bed
And write my life as a poem
Full of small agonies and possible insanity.
I'm proud of my narrow escape;
Much more slowly I crossed the tape.

But Life is a long-distance race,
And I am older than seventy
A remote grandfather of three across a big country.
It's hard to keep up the pace or stay ahead
Of Durer's Fate disguised in a viral shape,
Astride a Chinese saddle,
Riding an American horse into battle.

Though my lungs sit free from phlegm now
I'm filled with fear and anxiety for my little family.
Give me the breath for one last escape
Let me cross this tape faster than Fate.

A Poem's Last Gift

It's only a toy you pull on the ground
It has a lip that goes clack against the axle
And a face like a duck
It makes promises with a sound
You pull on the string and it follows along
From one room to the next
From birth until the end of your life.

It might be a bomb that never explodes
Or the song of an entire nation
It means everything and costs nothing
Or means nothing and costs everything.

FOR I HAVE NEGLECTED TO PRAISE
—*after Christopher Smart*

For I am filled with doom
and one with petulance.

For I am the first to complain
and rub my back in soreness.

For I am forgetful of pleasure
which lasts a moment.

For I am the first to wake in anger
and the last to sleep in peace.

For I am cautioned by bare branches
and wounded trees.

For I am blinded by every sunrise
and chilled by a setting sun.

For I am challenged by the ocean
and bored in quiet pools.

For I am churned by stain
and impatient of perfect beauty.

For I am pricked by premonition
and saddened by the birth of angels.

For I am deaf to promise
and envy confirmation.

For my poems are filled with grievance
and my letters cut open by grief.

For I am replete with doubt and disbelief
and have lost what once was found.

Acknowledgements

Grateful acknowledgement is made to the editors of the following literary magazines where most of the poems were first published, sometimes slightly altered:

Abandoned Mine: The Doctor Who Treats Himself Has a Fool for a Patient & Cat in Quarantine

Barrow Street Review: The House as a Lady and Where Guests Once Slept, from Eight Rooms for an Old House, and Correspondence: Deep Yellow—Green

Blood & Thunder: Evolution & The Surgeon, and In the O.R.

Broad River Review: Forensic Book Report

Burningword: Not Like a Poem

Concho River Review: Reflective Sonnet & Books on the Firing Range

Copihue: Ultimate Disappointment

Deep South Magazine: Pool Poem [4]: Coda & After Some Sayings by Rabbi Earl Grollman

Delmarva Review: The Bricks of Baltimore & A Bay Fisherman's Meteorological Lesson

Delta Poetry Review: Objects Removed for Study

Deronda Review: Augenblick is German for Glimpse

Euphony (U. Chicago): The Stack

Evening Street Review: Blue Smoke Inside My Head

Flare Journal: A Cold Chemical Light Gives Warning

Free State: Mosquito Erotica

Ginosko Literary Review: The Torch of Enthusiasm

Glimpse: The Original Glimpser & The Voice of Summer

Glint: A Sonnet Plus One About the Brain

Grey Sparrow Journal: A Dream of Morden Tower

Grounds Journal: The Importance of Measure

Gyroscope Review: Quarreling, For Us, Was A Kind of Intimacy

The Healing Muse: At the Universal

Helix: Autopsy

Hole in the Head Review: Bar Talk / Bartok & The Rainbow is the Enemy of Envy

The Hudson Review: Ascriptive

I-70 Review: A Day on the Big Island

Innisfree Poetry Journal: Outside in My Underwear

The Lake (UK): The Paper, The Difference Example Makes & Searching

Last Stanza Poetry Journal: Dinosaurs & Polio, 1952, and Jo in The Light

Little Patuxent Review: Built to Be Mute: The Pause

Loch Raven Review: Convergence of the Dead & Hard-Boiled Dicks

Lumina: Painted Lions Catch on Fire

The MacGuffin: Building a Prize-Winner

Medicine and Meaning: Aboard Sirène in the Morning

New Plains Review: Mother at Eighty-Eight

New York Quarterly: At the Keyboard (Kaddish) & Apocalypse

The Nonconformist: Dust in the Street

Orchards Poetry Review: Bittersweet

Pensive: A Poem's Last Gift (Perhaps)

Plainsongs: Same is Always Now

Red Ogre Review (UK): The Problem Is—

Relief: A Journal of the Arts & Faith: Catechism

Rockford Review: Pool Poem [1]: A Daisy Chain of Pools & *Sonomama* or My Wife's Flowers.

Salt: The Long Moment

The Same: New Yorkers

Sequestrum: Travesties of Aging

Slant: For I Have Neglected to Praise

Smartish Pace: Missing the Superfluous

South Florida Poetry Journal: The Last Jew in Kabul & The List

Stillwater: After the Surfside Tower Collapses & The Envelope

Thieving Magpie: Crossing the Tape, Earworms &The Vanished World of Iryna Abramov

Tipton Poetry Journal: The Coup & Gratitude

White Cresset Arts Journal: Hurricane Arthur

The Woven Tale: Hopper's Rooms by the Sea (1951)

Young Ravens Literary Review: In This House

"Correspondence: Deep Yellow—Green" was first published in the *Barrow Street Review* and collected in the New Poems section of my book *Necessary Speech: New & Selected Poems*, Spuyten Duyvil, New York, 2022.

"The Fire Inside Your Head" (Image 29) and "Blue Smoke Inside My Head" (Image 45) were collected by Julia Prendergast for the Australasian Association of Writing Programs (AAWP) and the Science Art Network (ScAN), and published in *The Writing Mind, Creative Writing Responses to Images of the Living Brain*, Julia Prendergast, Eileen Herbert-Goodall & Jen Webb (editors), Recent Work Press, Canberra, 2023

Sequestrum reprinted "The Long Moment", "The Torch of Enthusiasm", & "Missing the Superfluous" (2023)

"Dinosaurs & Polio, 1952" won the Editor's Choice Award from *Last Stanza Poetry Journal* (2022)

The Pool Poems (Nos.1 through 4) first appeared as "Swimming Lessons."

"The Paper" first appeared in *The Lake* (UK) as "I Will Go Down with the Ship."

"A Bay Fisherman's Meteorological Lesson" was reprinted by *The Talbot Spy* and its associated newspaper network on the Chesapeake Bay (2023)

This book of New Poems includes three much older ones: "Apocalypse" first drafted November, 1973, "Two Modern Architects" from 2004, and "New Yorkers" in 2007.

Notes on the Poems:

p.7 frontispiece: Leon Polk Smith (1906-1996), born to indigenous parents in the Oklahoma Territory, pioneer of hard-edge abstract painting who revived the shaped canvas. My ekphrastic poem is a rare example of an abstract poem about an abstract painting.

I

p.16 Olafur Eliasson (b.1967), one of the most popular conceptual artists of our time, often uses mirrors and lights to create visual environments; his laboratory is in Berlin.

p.18 Vin Scully moved with the Dodgers from Brooklyn to Los Angeles; he served as the greatest sportscaster and baseball raconteur of all time from 1950-2016.

II

p.33 the epigraph is by Milan Kundera (1929-2023), the Czech-French novelist and essayist.

p.35 the War to End all Wars ended the lives of many distinguished poets and visual artists, including Guillaume Apollinaire, Umberto Boccioni, Rupert Brooke, Raymond Duchamp-Villon, Henri Gaudier-Brzeska, August Macke, Franz Marc, Wilfred Owen, Isaac Rosenberg and Edward Thomas, a poet friend of Robert Frost.

p.37 Rabbi Earl Grollman (1925-2021), prolific writer and lecturer who often demystified Grief and Dying with clever and humorous sayings.

p.50 the epigraph is from "on weather" by Robert Hass (b.1941).

p.53 the final two lines by Kafka are from a 1904 letter he wrote to Oscar Pollack, a childhood friend, just after he finished reading the diaries of Christian Friedrich Hebbel, a German poet.

p.54 "Scrubbing off the past that cannot be scrubbed off" is from *Blizzard* by the American poet Henri Cole (b.1956)

III

p.55 Bernstein's famous quip as told to me by the Minimalist composer Philip Glass.

p.57 Walter Charleton (1619-1707), "a natural philosopher" and English writer, received his doctorate at age 22 and was appointed physician to Charles I the same year.

p.62 John Cheever (1912-1982) was one of America's finest short story writers.

p.65 tearing the olfactory nerves is one of the risks in retracting the brain to get to the neighborhood of the optic nerve; Proust made triggering olfactory memory famous.

p.71 the mathematical functions and symbols in this 15-liner are meant to be read out loud whenever this poem is performed.

IV

p.73 the epigraphs are by Marcel Proust (1871-1922), whose seven-volume masterpiece is filled with references to visual artists and musicians, both imaginary and real, and Simonides of Ceos (c.556-468 BCE), one of nine lyric poets esteemed by scholars in Hellenistic Alexandria.

p.77 my poem about Antoni Gaudi (1852-1926), "In Old Barcelona," is from *The Clock Made of Confetti* (2007); Louis Kahn (1901-1973), who designed a bizarre life-style for himself gave us jewels like Fort Worth's Kimbell Art Museum and the Yale Center for British Art.

p.83-84 realist paintings by Pieter Breughel the Elder and Edward Hopper (1882-1967) are the most common subjects for ekphrastic poems; I felt addicted doing just two of the latter.

p.85 the Hungarian Béla Bartók (1881-1945), one of the great composers of the 20th century, briefly escaped the war in the United States and died of cancer in New York.

p.88 Salvador Dalí (1904-1989) often made use of burning lions and fires as surrealist symbols; the second stanza makes reference to Einstein, Yeats and two other surrealists.

V
p.93 the title is a quote from *Ancient Light* by the Irish novelist John Banville (b.1945); twice a finalist for the Booker Prize, he won the second time with *The Sea* (2005).

p.96 the poem is dedicated to five major mentors and poet-friends of mine, three of whom (Daniel Hoffman, Dick Wilbur and Don Hall) served as US poet laureate and two who could have (Tom Lux and Dick Allen); they are frequently on my mind.

p.104 George Sanders (1906-1972), the actor who played the villain in *Laura* killed himself in real life and left a simple note that said "I am leaving because I am bored."

p.107 Sir William Osler, one of history's earliest scientific physicians, very quotable and a member of the Big Four involved in founding the Johns Hopkins School of Medicine.

p.112 The famous woodcut of *The Four Horsemen of the Apocalypse* (1498) was cut and printed by the finest artist of the Renaissance outside Italy, Albrecht Durer (1471-1528).

p.114 based on a poem by Christopher Smart (1722-1771), a visionary poet and precursor to the English Romantic movement, who authored the best literary tribute to a pet "For I Will Consider My Cat Jeoffrey," an anaphoric section in *Jubilate Agno*, first published in 1939.

WITH GRATITUDE

Artists tend to suffer from a certain amount of insecurity. For this reason, writers of books need to be lucky in their friends, whether they be close readers or good listeners. More than any of my other collections, *Crossing the Tape* owes much of its final sound and shape to my dear friend David Bergman, poet, essayist and emeritus professor of English at Towson University. Similarly, many early drafts of the poems found their way to Robert Cooperman, a gifted poet and childhood friend. Enthusiastic responses by Lee Boot, an experimental media artist, professor and director of the Imaging Center at UMBC, University of Maryland Baltimore County, to several new and as yet unpublished poems in journals caused me to include them in the book (not my usual modus operandi). I am especially grateful to Francine Krumholz, another long-time friend, for bringing me the war-time diary of her uncle. Other cherished listeners have included neighbors like Bill and Jane Sieglein and, as always, my remarkable wife Ilene Salcman. Further readers of the poems in Baltimore include poets Shirley Brewer and Gregg Mosson. In New York, over several years, a number of the poems have been read to poet members of our group Poetry@theCentury, among them Elizabeth Coleman, Margaret Douglas-Hamilton, and Owen Lewis, as well as Helen Houghton, anthologist and life-time student of verse, who keeps me and our members organized. *Crossing the Tape* is my third book of poems at Spuyten Duyvil; I am very grateful to Tod Thilleman, my deeply understanding publisher, and Joshua Salcman, my wonderful son, who has designed such beautiful covers for my books.

MICHAEL SALCMAN, poet, physician and art historian, was born in Pilsen, Czechoslovakia, came to the United States in 1949 and trained in neurosurgery at Columbia University. Formerly chair of neurosurgery at the University of Maryland and president of the Contemporary Museum in Baltimore, he is the author of six medical textbooks and nine previous collections of poems, including *The Clock Made of Confetti*, nominated for The Poets' Prize, *The Enemy of Good is Better*, and *A Prague Spring, Before & After*, winner of the 2015 Sinclair Poetry Prize. He edited *Poetry in Medicine*, a standard anthology of classic and contemporary poems about doctors, patients, illness and healing. His poems appear in prominent journals including *Alaska Quarterly Review, Arts & Letters, Barrow Street, Harvard Review, Hopkins Review, Hudson Review, New Letters, Ontario Review, Poet Lore, Raritan* and *Smartish Pace*. In 2020, *Shades & Graces: New Poems*, was the inaugural winner of the Daniel Hoffman Legacy Book Prize. His next collection, *Necessary Speech: New & Selected Poems* was published by Spuyten Duyvil in 2022.

www.ingramcontent.com/pod-product-compliance
Lightning Source LLC
Chambersburg PA
CBHW031429120626
46545CB00006B/2328